Table of Contents

Introduction

A nice noodle is loved by everyone, and these chunky egg twists which originate in Swabia, on the south-western border of Germany, should be more recognized here. Had it not been that our knowledge of the country's cuisine begins and stops with the Black Forest gateau.

In neighboring Hungary, Eastern France, Austria even the Italian province of South Tyrol, variations of the theme are eaten. Only the Swabian spätzle is recognized by the EU having a Protected Indication Geographically for their quality.

These delicate noodles are so versatile. There is hardly a dish that cannot be enhanced, served or transformed with a good helping of these noodles. They can be tossed with greens or drenched with gravy; it is considerably easier and quicker to make than Italian pasta.

These recipes are guaranteed to improve your life.

German Spätzle Dumplings

Special German Dumplings can be made more delicious with the addition of bacon.

Serves:6

Time: 8 mins.

Ingredients:

- eggs (2)
- flour (1 cup)
- milk (¼ cup)
- nutmeg (½ teaspoon)
- pepper (1 pinch)
- salt (½ teaspoon)
- butter (2 tbsp)
- parsley (2 tbsp)

Directions:

1. Whisk eggs and add milk gradually while keep whisking. Add flour, white pepper, salt and nutmeg into the mixture while mixing quickly till smooth.

2. Press the dough with a metal grater or large holed sieve.

3. At a time, put few dumplings into boiling water for 5 to 8 minutes and drain well.

4. Put cooked spätzle in a pan and sauté in butter or margarine. Garnish with chopped parsley and serve hot.

German Spätzle with Sauerkraut 2

Butter sautéed homemade traditional spätzle with sauerkraut and breadcrumbs will be a great treat for your taste buds.

Serves:6

Time: 15 mins.

Ingredients:

- oil (1 tablespoon)
- eggs (8)
- salt (1 tablespoon)
- flour (4 ½ cups)
- butter (½ cup)
- sauerkraut (1 can)
- breadcrumbs (4 tablespoons)

Directions:

1. Put a large water filled pan on heat, add some oil and bring to boil.

2. Knead a smooth, thick and bubbly dough with flour, eggs, salt and water. Put dough in spätzle maker and squeeze into the boiling water (Colander can be used to push the dough through).

3. Drain spätzle well after the float on top of boiling water. In a glass baking dish, put half of spätzle and place a layer of sauerkraut and repeat this layering process. To keep the dish warm covered it.

4. Add breadcrumbs in melted butter in a separate pan and let them become moist. Sprinkle breadcrumbs on top. Serve this layered dish. Add some butter while reheating the next day.

Homemade Spätzle I

Enjoy the treat of Homemade Spätzle

Serves:4

Time: 5 mins.

Ingredients:

- eggs (2 large)
- flour (all-purpose, 3 cups)
- Kosher salt
- unsalted butter (2 tablespoons, melted)
- Finely ground pepper
- Freshly chopped parsley

Directions:

1. Add the flour, eggs, and a bit of salt in a cup of water and stir well to make a smooth batter like a dough.

2. After the formation of bubbles, add in the melted butter and stir well.

3. Fill a large saucepan with salted water and boil. Fill dough in spätzl maker and press dough.

4. Squeeze in boiling water and cook for 1 minute and drain well. Repeat process with the remaining dough.

5. If not serving immediately, rinse spätzle with cold water and set aside.

6. In a skillet, sauté spätzle in remaining 2 tablespoons of butter till warm enough. Before serving, garnish with parsley and season with pepper.

Spätzle noodles

Unique idea to make perfect homemade spätzle noodles.

Serves:6

Time: 20 mins.

Ingredients:

- eggs (4 beaten large)
- flour (3 cups of unbleached)
- salt (1 teaspoon)
- nutmeg (1/4 teaspoon)
- water (1/2 cup)
- butter (1/4 cup)

Directions:

1. In a bowl, mix flour, nutmeg, and salt together.

2. Pour ¼ cup of water and eggs into the center of flour mixture and beat

well.

3. To make the dough sticky, yet elastic and stiff, add some water.

4. With spätzle machine or a medium holed colander press your noodles into a large pan of salted boiling water.

5. For 5 minutes' cook noodles or till they rise to the surface.

6. Take out noodles and put on paper towels.

7. Over low heat let the noodles in melted butter.

Kaese Spätzle

The mouthwatering German macaroni dish will definitely fill your tummy.

Serves:8

Time: 20 mins.

Ingredients:

- eggs (3)
- salt (¾ teaspoons)
- nutmeg (3/4 tsp)
- pepper (3/4 tsp)
- flour (1 ½ cups)
- onion (1)
- milk (3/8 cups)
- butter (3 tablespoons)
- cheese (1 ½ cups)

Directions:

1. Sift flour, salt, pepper and nutmeg together. In a bowl whisk eggs.

2. Mix in milk and the flour mixture well till smooth. Let it stand for 25 minutes.

3. Boil a large pan of salted water. Fill batter in spätzle and press into the water.

4. Potato ricer, colander, or a cheese grater can also be used. Drain spätzle well when floating on water and mix in 1 cup of cheese.

5. Cook onion till golden in a skillet, add in butter and put spätzle and remaining cheese and blend well.

6. Serve immediately after removing from heat.

Spätzle with Chicken Soup

These delicious homemade noodles cooked with frozen chicken breast if you don't have time to use a whole chicken

Serves:8

Time: 2 hrs.

Ingredients:

- chicken (3 pound)
- chicken broth (15 ounce)
- onions (2 medium, quartered yellow)
- celery (1 bunch, cut into pieces)
- carrots (1 package, 16 ounce)
- Salt and ground black pepper (to taste)
- eggs (5 large)
- garlic salt (1/2 teaspoons)

- salt (1 teaspoon)
- water (1/2 cup)
- parsley flakes (1/2 teaspoon)
- all-purpose flour (3 cups)

Directions:

1. Make broth by putting chicken in pot and cover chicken with water. Add celery, onions, salt, garlic salt and pepper and boil for 1 hour.

2. Strain broth, discard celery and onion and shred chicken after cooling. Add shredded chicken in broth and add carrots, boil.

3. Whisk eggs, salt and water in a bowl and add flour gradually to make a ball shaped firm dough. Roll dough on flat plate and cut 2 to 3 inches long strips of dough and directly make them fall into the boiling broth.

4. Soup is ready to serve when carrots are tender, garnish with parsley.

Kaes-Spazle

Salad in a sour dressing will go well with this relishing vegetarian dish from Bavaria and Baden-Württemberg.

Serves: 4

Time: 15 mins.

Ingredients:

- eggs (3 large)
- all-purpose flour (1 3/4 cups)
- water (3/4 cup)
- vegetable oil (1 tablespoon)
- vegetable oil (1/4 cup)
- salt (1/4 cup)
- onions (2 large, sliced)
- Swiss cheese (3 cups of shredded)
- parsley (1 tsp, freshly, chopped)
- vinegar (1 tbsp, white)

- Add these Ingredients to list

Directions:

1. Mix flour, eggs, one tablespoon oil, salt and ½ cup of water in a bowl until smooth.

2. Rest for 10 minutes. Over medium heat in a skillet, heat ¼ cup of oil.

3. Sauté onion slices till golden brown and set aside. Preheat oven at 300 degrees F (150 degrees C).

4. In a large pan, boil salted water. Fill the dough in spätzle and press.

5. Let the spätzle directly drop into boiling water. Drain and put them in 9inch casserole dish.

6. Spread them well and cover with 1/3 of cheese. Repeat the layering process and top with fried onions.

7. Bake for 15 minutes in preheated oven till the cheese melts thoroughly.

8. Before serving, sprinkle 2 tablespoons of vinegar and chopped parsley.

Herb Spätzle

Non-traditional seasoning makes this dish the yummiest one.

Serves: 6

Time: 10 mins.

Ingredients:

- all-purpose flour (4 cups)
- powdered onion (1 tbsp)
- basil (2 tablespoons, dried)
- Grounded black pepper and salt for taste
- eggs (5 large)
- water (4 cups)
- water (1 ¾ cups)
- salt (2 tablespoons)

Directions:

1. Whisk eggs in 1 ¾ cups of water in a bowl. Combine basil, flour, onion powder, salt and black pepper in a large bowl.

2. Create a hole in the middle of flour mix and pour egg mixt into it. Stir well and make a thick dough.

3. In a wide pan boil 4 cups of salted water. Fill dough into a spätzle maker and press into boiling water.

4. Stir pasta well till tender. Remove the pasta using a slotted spoon to a large bowl.

Papa Oriold's Spätzle

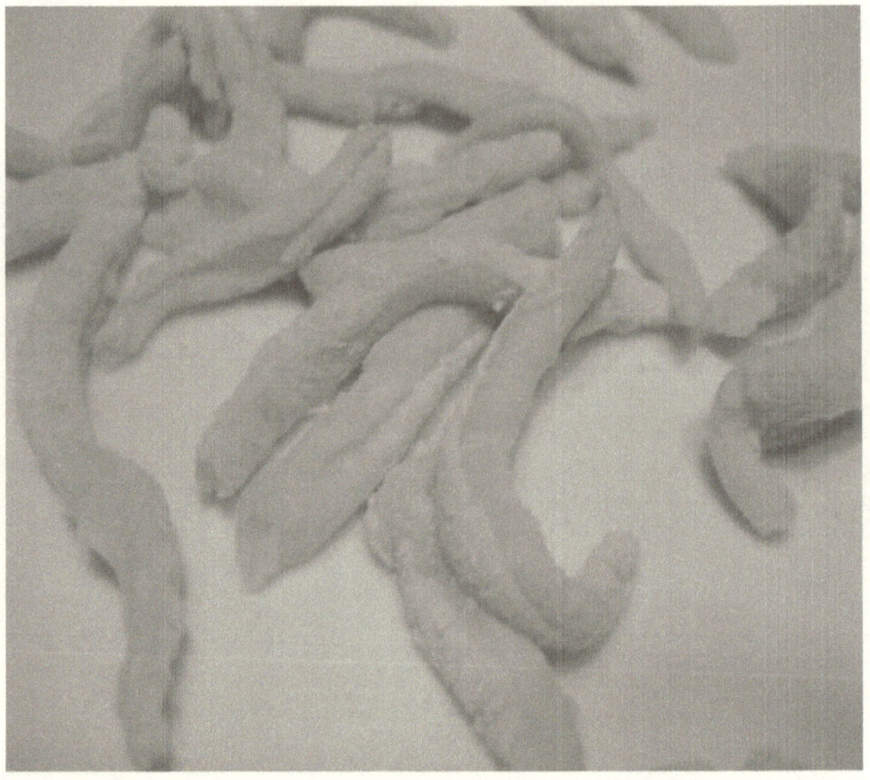

Soup or chicken paprikash will complement this fluffy spätzle.

Serves:4

Time: 15 mins.

Ingredients:

- all-purpose flour (3 cups)
- eggs (5 large, beaten)
- water (1 cup, cold)
- salt (1 tsp)
- baking powder (1/4 teaspoon)

Directions:

1. Mix and blend water, eggs, flour, baking powder and salt in a bowl.

2. Fill a wide pot with water and boil. Put part of dough into potato ricer or spätzle maker and press the dough directly in the boiling water, cook while stirring and let the pasta float for about 2 minutes. Remove and rinse pasta with water.

Spätzle, Sauerkraut with Sausage Casserole

This filling dish can also be served the next day after reheating.

Serves: 6

Time: 55 mins.

Ingredients:

- all-purpose flour (1 1/3 cups)
- eggs (3 large)
- salt (1 teaspoon)
- water (1/3 cup)
- vegetable oil (1 teaspoon)
- bacon (2 slices, diced)
- onion (1/2 large, chopped)
- gala apple (1 cored and chopped)
- brown sugar (2 tablespoons)
- butter (2 tablespoons)
- sauerkraut (1 package)

- A kielbasa sausage package and cut into 2-inch pieces

Directions:

1. Preheat oven to 175 degrees C.

2. Mix eggs and water and whisk well. In a bowl, mix together flour and salt. Forming a dough by pouring the egg to mix well.

3. Boil water in a big pot. Put oiled colander over the water pot and fill spätzle dough into the colander, push the dough with a flexible spatula into the boiling water.

4. Scoop the spätzle after 5 minutes and place them on a baking dish which is an ungreased 9x9 inch.

5. In the skillet, cook bacon for 8 minutes over a medium heat. Place bacon in a plate and cook onions in the bacon dripping until brown for 10 minutes.

6. Melt butter over medium heat till foamy and stir brown sugar and apples in a large skillet. Cook while stirring for 5 minutes.

7. Put cooked bacon, sauerkraut and onions in the skillet and stir occasionally for 5 minutes to blend the flavors. Pour this mixture on top of 9x9 inch spätzle baking dish.

8. Put sausage into the microwave safe dish and cook on the full power until sausages lose their pink color.

9. Put the sausage in the baking dish and bake for 15 minutes until bubbling.

Roasted Chicken with Port and Cherries on the Buttered Spätzle

This classic combo of chicken and cherries in a dark port wine sauce with homemade spätzle in brown butter will win everyone's heart.

Serves:6

Time: 35 mins.

Ingredients:

- milk (3/4 cup, whole)
- eggs (3 large)
- salt (1 teaspoon)
- nutmeg (1/4 teaspoon, ground)
- flour (2 cups, all purpose)
- chicken breast (6 (5 ounce) of boneless, halves with skin)

- flour (1 cup, all purpose)
- kosher salt (1 teaspoon)
- white pepper (1/3 teaspoon)
- unsalted butter (6 tablespoons)
- olive oil (3 tablespoons)
- chicken livers (1 pound trimmed and halved)
- Bing cherries (3/4 cup of dried)
- port wine (1 cup)
- chicken stock (1 1/2 cups of brown)
- cornstarch (1 tablespoon)
- water (1 tablespoon of cold)
- unsalted butter (1/2 cup)

Directions:

1. Mix eggs, salt, milk and nutmeg in a blender and blend for 30 seconds. Add flour and blend for 30 seconds to make a thick and sticky batter.

2. Make salted water in a pot and boil. In a potato ricer, put some batter and press to form strands.

3. To avoid sticking, stir them while they hit the water. Remove them with a slotted spoon when they start floating to the surface of water.

4. Put them into a large greased baking dish. Do this for 2 hours in advance and keep them at room temperature.

5. Mix flour, salt and pepper on a paper plate. Coat the chicken in the mixture and dust off the excess. Melt butter on the medium heat in a skillet.

6. Put in olive oil. When bubbling, start adding chicken with skin side down. After it gets golden brown, turn the other side and cook in the same way.

7. Take out the chicken in a platter and to keep it warm cover it with aluminum foil.

8. In another skillet, heat 2 tablespoons of butter and 1 tablespoon of olive oil over medium high heat.

9. Put the chicken livers and cook without stirring for about 2 minutes each side.

10. Put the livers in the chicken platter, while still pink in the middle.

11. With paper towel, clean the first skillet. Add one tablespoon of olive oil and 2 tablespoons of butter and heat till bubbly and hot over medium high heat.

12. Put port wine, chicken stock and cherries and bring it to simmer. Reduce by one third. Mix corn starch in cold water and pour it into the sauce.

13. Stir the sauce until thickened. Put skin side up chicken breasts and tilt the pan and pour sauce over them. Also put chicken livers and coat them with the sauce well. Turn the heat very slow.

14. In a large skillet, melt 1/2 cup of butter on medium heat until golden brown (3 minutes). Put spätzle and toss well. Season with salt and pepper.

15. Top the pile spätzle with chicken and sauce. Ready to serve.

Homemade Spätzle's II

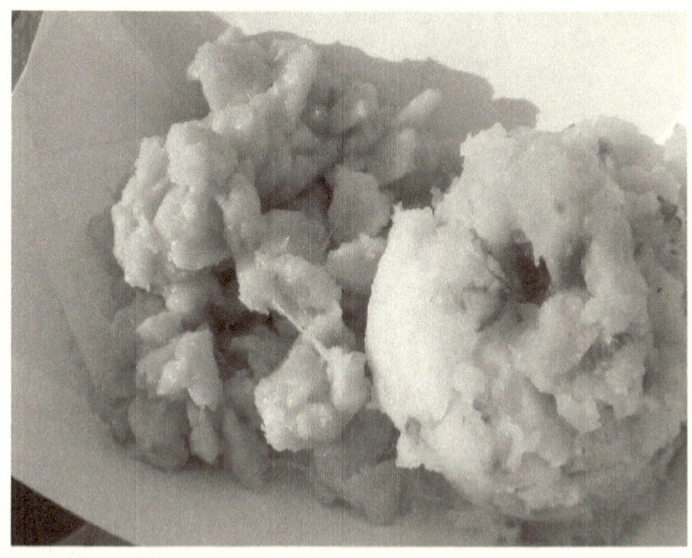

Amazingly, these noodles can be frozen after cooking.

Serves:4

Time: 15 mins.

Ingredients:

- flour (1 cup)
- eggs (2)

Directions:

1. In a medium bowl, put flour and make a well. Pour eggs and mix with a fork.

2. Knead well to form a stiff dough. With the help of your fingers, pinch off half inch pieces of batter and directly put them in boiling water.

3. Cook till the dumplings float to the surface (5-15 minutes).

Bacon Onion Spätzle

Perfect blend of flavors in this smoky bacon invites the hungry tummies.

Serves:6

Time: 30 mins.

Ingredients:

- flour (2 cups of all-purpose)
- salt (1/4 teaspoon)
- nutmeg (1/4 teaspoon, ground)
- eggs (3 lightly, beaten)
- milk (1 cup)
- bacon (1/4 lbs., diced smoked)
- onion (1 chopped yellow)
- olive oil (1 tablespoon)

- Freshly chopped parsley
- Freshly ground black pepper and kosher salt

Directions:

1. Mix salt, nutmeg and flour in a medium bowl. Combine egg and milk in a separate bowl.

2. Add in the dry mixture and knead the smooth dough. Let it rest for 30 minutes.

3. With the help of a sieve, press the dough over boiling salted water.

4. Cook the spätzle for about 1 minute. Remove cooked spätzle and put them in ice water. Drain and set aside.

5. Cook bacon for 4-5 minutes in a skillet over a medium heat. Put onions and cook them about 4-5 minutes. In another pan, put some oil and sauté the cooked spätzle until golden.

6. Mix in the battered mixture and season them with salt and pepper, and garnish with parsley.

Crumb-Coated Spätzle

This old time German spätzle will enhance the taste of all types of roasts.

Serves:6

Time: 5 mins.

Ingredients:

- flour (2 cups, all purpose)
- salt (1 tsp)
- eggs (2, lightly, beaten)
- milk (3/4 cup, 2%)
- breadcrumbs (1/2 cup, dried)
- butter (1/2 cup, melted)

Directions:

1. Beat eggs and milk until smooth and combine salt and flour into it.

2. Boil the water in a large pan. Then press dough through a colander with a rubber spatula into boiling water. Stir gently and cook for 4 minutes till it

floats and is tender.

3. Mix butter and breadcrumbs and add the mixture onto spätzle and it is ready to serve.

Ham and Spätzle Bake

This ready-to-eat creamy and cheesy meat dish has no other parallel.

Serves:2

Time: 15 mins.

Ingredients:

- spätzle (3/4 cup, uncooked)
- onion (1/3 cup of finely)
- butter (2 tsp)
- flour (2 tsp, all purpose)
- milk (1/2 cup)
- broccoli florets (3/4 cup of fresh)
- Gruyere cheese (1/3 cup of shredded)
- deli ham (1/3 cup of cubed)
- mustard (1/2 teaspoon of ground)
- pepper (1/8 teaspoon of)

Directions:

1. Cook spätzle as the package Directions. Sauté onion in butter till tender.

2. Add the flour and stir into a small saucepan, gradually pour milk. Stir and bring to boil, cook until thickened.

3. Remove from the heat. Mix spätzle, cheese broccoli, mustard, ham and pepper into white sauce.

4. Transfer the mixture into a greased baking dish.

5. At 375° bake while uncovered for 15-18 minutes or until bubbly.

Cheese Spätzle

Easy-to-cook dumplings will draw everyone to the dining table.

Serves:2

Time: 12 mins.

Ingredients:

- flour (1 cup, all purpose)
- salt (1 tsp)
- black pepper (1/2 teaspoon)
- Gruyère cheese (1/3 cup)
- eggs (2)
- milk (1/4 cup)
- butter (3 tablespoons, unsalted)
- parsley (2 tbsp, chopped)

Directions:

1. Beat milk and eggs into a small bowl, in a bowl, mix salt, pepper, flour and

half of the cheese.

2. Make a well in the dry Ingredients and pour the egg mixture. Gradually combine the mixture and make smooth and thick dough. Rest the dough for 10-15 minutes.

3. In the meantime, put salted water in a large pot and bring the water to boil over high heat.

4. Let the water simmer over low heat. Set a big holed colander over the simmering water.

5. Fill dough into the colander and push the dough with the help of a ladle or rubber spatula into the water and cook for 3-4 minutes till the spätzle becomes tender.

6. Transfer the spätzle with small strainer into a larger strainer and drain it well and rinse it with cold water.

7. Over medium high heat, melt the butter in a large frying pan. Add spätzle and toss well to coat evenly, cook for about 8 minutes till half the spätzles are browned.

Oma cheese spat

Now you can easily make them at home. In fact, it tastes far better than those available in markets.

Serves:4

Time: 30 mins.

Ingredients:

- onions (2 small sized, thinly sliced)
- Spätzle (3 to 4 cups of cooked)
- Emmental cheese (2 to 3 cups of shredded)
- melted butter (2 tbsp)
- olive oil.

Directions:

1. Heat up oven at the 325F temperature.

2. In a pan, add oil or butter and let it heat for some moments. Now add onions and cook them for 5 to 10 minutes until their color changes into brown.

3. Simmer dish with butter. Now apply first layer of Spätzle and sprinkle pepper salt and shredded cheese over it.

4. Go on applying layers along with cheese in them.

5. Garnish its top with browned onions.

6. Put it in oven as it is and bake.

Goulash

Instead of going to the market and buying your favorite dish at a high price, let's make it at home.

Serves:6

Time: 1 hr.

Ingredients:

- pepper and salt (Half tsp)
- tomato paste (1 tbsp)
- bay leaf (1)
- oil or butter (3 tbsp)
- red wine (3 tbsp)
- beef chunks or cubes (3 lbs.,)
- beef broth (2 cups)
- garlic clove (1, properly minced, optional)
- Hungarian paprika (1 to 2 tbsp. sweet)
- Onions (3 to 4 finely chopped)

- Carrots (2, sliced)

Directions:

1. Add butter to a pan and cook beef chunks over high flame. When its color changes, and properly cooked, put them in a bowl.

2. Now add garlic and onions and fry them for 5 minutes on a medium flame.

3. Add cooked beef chunks and remaining ingredients.

4. Cook them until soup boils. Now reduce flame and keep it covered.

5. Cook it for at least one and half hour so that meat is tender.

Schupfnudeln

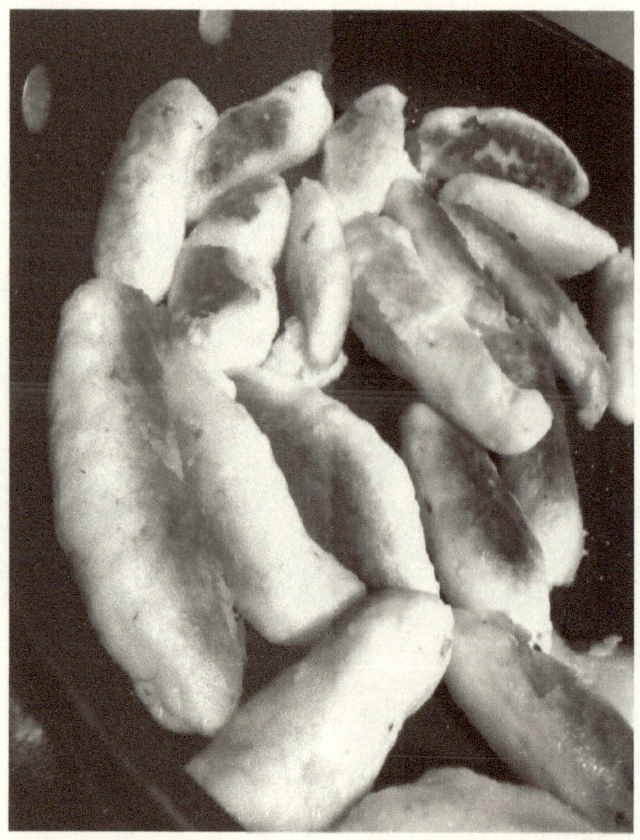

One of the most popular side dishes which is not only made in Baden-Wurttemberg but cooked all over Germany.

Serves:4

Time: 10 mins.

Ingredients:

- Butter (2 tbsp.)
- corn starch (2 tbsp.)
- eggs (2)
- Salt, nutmeg and pepper.
- Potatoes (1 lb. peeled and cubed)
- Flour (4 tbsp)

Directions:

1. Boil potatoes in water.

2. When they are fully tender, let them dry.

3. Completely mash potatoes and add cornstarch, eggs and flour. Make a puree.

4. Now sprinkle nutmeg powder, salt and pepper to a taste.

5. Apply some flour on your hands. Make a dough and roll it in order to form a long rod like structure. Now make 19 to 20 pieces and roll each piece in both of your hands to form thin finger shapes. It must have pointed narrow endings with middle part thicker.

6. Boil some water and add these shapes in it. Gently boil them for only 5 minutes. Take them out and drain water from them.

7. Melt butter in a saucepan. Stir fry potato noodles until their color changes.

Baked Spaghetti

Most quick and easy recipe which is also very demanding can now be made for dinners at home. It is commonly known as "aka Uberbackene Spaghetti".

Serves:4

Time: 10 mins.

Ingredients:

- thyme (1 tbsp)
- peppers (3, different colors)
- Salt and pepper.
- Spaghetti (10 oz)
- Gouda (8 oz. sliced)
- olive oil (2 tbsp)
- garlic clove (1)

Directions:

1. Boil spaghetti and drain out water.

2. Heat up oven at 425F.

3. Cook peppers in oil for 5 minutes.

4. Add other Ingredients and boiled spaghetti.

5. Grease a dish and add mixture in it with cheese and thyme topping.

6. Bake it for 10 minutes.

German Noodle Nest

Instead of noodles Germans go for spaghetti in it. So, you can enjoy colors of culture along with its fabulous taste.

Serves:6

Time: 30 mins.

Ingredients:

- Salt and pepper.
- spaghetti (12 oz)
- mozzarella (4 oz, cubed)
- olive oil (5 tbsp)
- onions (3 chopped)
- pasta sauce (24 oz)
- garlic clove (1 pasted).
- Sausage (2-3 smoked)
- mushrooms (1 lb.)

Directions:

1. Heat up oven at 400F. 2. Boil spaghetti and wash them with cold water. Then add oil.

2. Cut mushrooms and stir fry them in oil along with sausages. Add garlic paste, cook for few minutes and turn of stove.

3. Now add salt & pepper and onions. Grease dish with pasta sauce.

4. Make a nest of spaghetti in a pan using fork. Add mushroom mixture in depression.

5. Pour remaining pasta sauce. Spread cheese over it. Bake for half an hour.

Jaeger Schnitzel

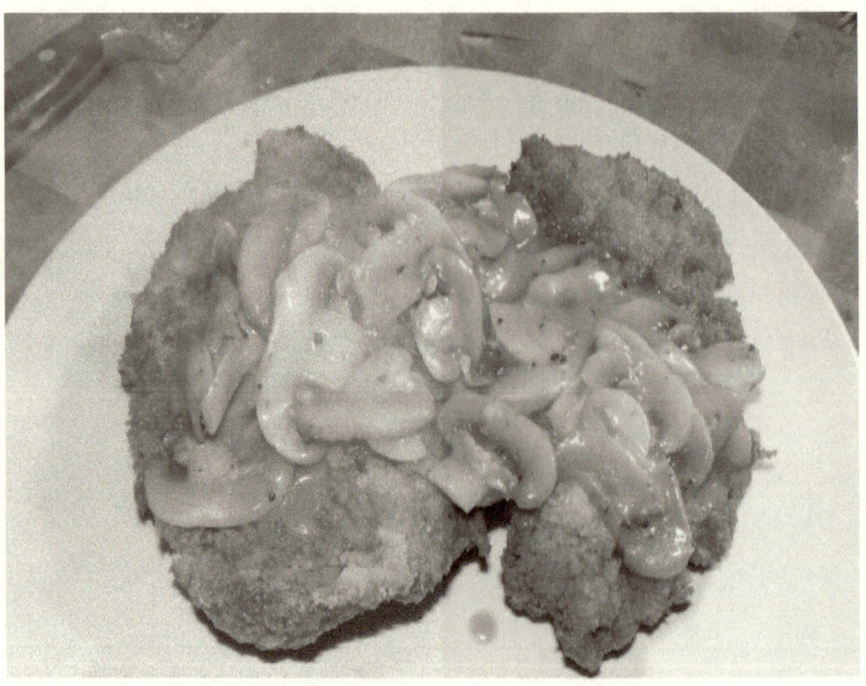

This sauce is best for the spätzle dishes.

Serves:4

Time: 35 mins.

Ingredients:

- flour (¼ cup)
- butter (1 tablespoon)
- beef broth (2 ½ cups)
- shallot (¼ cup, mined)
- salt (¼ teaspoon)
- mushrooms (3 cups)

Directions:

1. Melt the butter and sauté the shallots. Fry the mushrooms in butter.

2. Put flour in a bowl and whisk the beef broth gradually.

3. Put the broth in mushrooms and boil for 10 minutes to make a thick mixture.

Geschnetzeltes

The delicious meaty sauce with spätzle.

Serves:4

Time: 25 mins.

Ingredients:

- onion (1)
- lean pork
- mushrooms (8 lb.,)
- olive oil (2 tablespoons)
- butter (3 tablespoons)
- milk (1 cup)
- flour (3 tablespoons)
- heavy milk (1 cup)
- paprika (1 tablespoon)
- beef bouillon (2 cubes)
- Spätzle (1 pack)

Directions:

1. Take a pan and put oil in it. Heat it at medium flame and fry pork in it. Put it aside in a plate.

2. Add in onions and sauté for 7 minutes.

3. Add in mushrooms and stir further for 5 minutes.

4. Add butter in a pan and whisk the flour. Add cream and milk and whisk constantly.

5. In beef stock, add paprika and mix well.

6. Simmer the meat mixture and add in milk, pepper and salt to thicken.

7. Add meat mixture to the sauce, cover and simmer. Season with salt and pepper. Serve with hot spätzle.

Mutti Salad

The famous German salad to be served with spätzle.

Serves: 3

Time: 0 mins.

Ingredients:

- herring (1 jar)
- dill pickles (4)
- sour cream (½ cup)

Directions:

1. Mix cream with herrings. Include the dill pickles and mix further. Serve instantly.

Riffles

The most favorite noodle mixture with broth.

Serves: 3

Time: 15 mins.

Ingredients:

- Egg noodles
- egg (1)
- flour (1 cup)
- milk (2 tablespoons)
- sea salt (1/2 teaspoon)
- Chicken broth
- garlic (½ teaspoon)
- chicken broth (8 cups)
- chicken breasts (2)
- salt (1/4 tsp)

- pepper (1/2 teaspoon)
- rosemary (1 teaspoon)
- milk (8 cups)

Directions:

1. Mix all the dry Ingredients into a bowl. **Add** a little milk

2. Let them dry for 20 minutes to form noodles.

3. Mix it with shredded chicken and spices. Cook for 15 minutes with stirring.

4. Serve hot.

German noodles

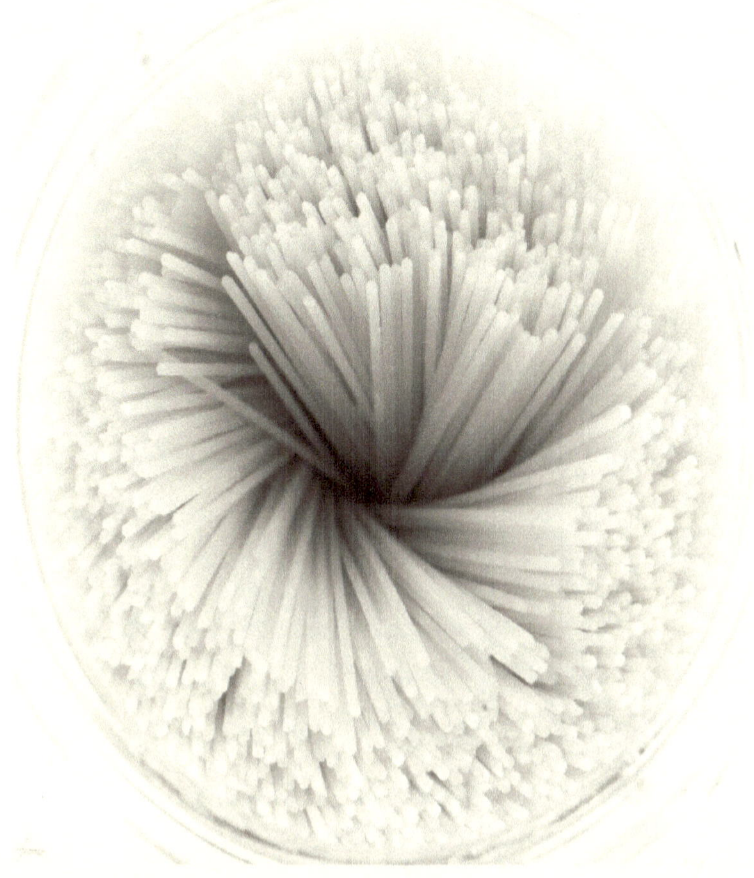

The easiest noodles known all around the state.

Serves:4

Time: 0 mins.

Ingredients:

- eggs (2)
- flour (2 ¼ cups)
- salt (1 tsp)
- water (1 cup)

Directions:

Mix salt and flour in the bowl

Add eggs and stir well.

Add water slowly to form firm dough.

Let it stand for 10 minutes

Make the noodles shape of this dough.

Serve with fried onions or meat.

Chocolate Spätzle

A delicious recipe which includes the amazing flavor of chocolate and strawberry, enriched with the creamy taste of crème fraiche.

Serves:3

Time: 15 mins.

Ingredients:

- Strawberry sorbet.
- Eggs (2)
- Olive oil.
- crème fraiche. (81/2 oz.)
- Chocolate Meringue.
- sugar. (1 oz.)
- flour. (7 oz.)
- vanilla extract. (2 tsp)
- Macerated strawberries.
- salt. (5 tsp)

- cocoa powder. (11/2 oz.)
- chocolate. (2 oz., semi melted)
- chocolate. (1 ½ oz., atomized)

Directions:

1. Blend eggs, vanilla extract, crème fraiche and melted chocolate together and make a puree.

2. Add up all dry components in a bowl and mix them.

3. Make a space in middle of bowl and pour puree in it. Let it rest of at least half an hour.

4. Take a pot containing boiling water and press the mixture well. Drain it after cooking for minimum 2 minutes. Pour it in a bowl and sprinkle a bit of salt and cover with olive oil.

5. Prepare your griddles. Now spread prepared spätzle along with macerated strawberries. Make crispy spätzle.

6. Garnish with strawberry sorbet and chocolate meringue.

Cinnamon Spätzle with Cranberries and Apples

One of the most famous sweet dish of Bavarian spätzle. It is also served as a side dish. It comes with the crusty flavor of the nuts and walnuts.

Serves:4

Time: 10 mins.

Ingredients:

- eggs. (4)
- vegetable oil
- flour (2 cups)
- kosher salt (1 tsp)
- cinnamon (2 tsp)
- vanilla extract (2 tsp)
- almond milk (1/3 cup

Directions:

1. Boil some water in a pot.

2. Mix cinnamon and flour. Take another bowl, add salt, milk, eggs and vanilla, whisk them together. Now mix two mixtures and keep it aside for 10 minutes.

3. Place spätzle maker on a boiling water after spraying with cooking spray.

4. Add above written mixture in it and stir it slowly. Slowly letting it to fall in boiling water.

5. Cook for 5 minutes. Drain it while rinsing with cold water.

6. Liquefy butter on medium flame. Mix up all above written cooked batter and cook until it turns brown. Serve it.

Swiss Apple Spätzle

A famous Swiss desert which is served with the spätzle recipes and includes the delicious flavor of fried and sweet apples with amazing topping of bread crust.

Serves:8

Time: 10 mins.

Ingredients:

For batter:

- Apples (2)
- Sugar (1 tbsp)
- Flour (7.5 oz. leveled plain)
- Eggs (2)

- kosher salt (2)

Finishing:

- cinnamon (¼ tsp)
- calvados (¼ cup)
- sugar (2 tsp)
- crumbs (1/3 cup homemade)
- lemon juice (1/2 tsp, fresh)
- butter (4 tbsp)

Directions:

1. Take apple and grate them wholesome. Don't squeeze out their juice as they will be used in the batter later.

2. Add salt, sugar and beaten eggs in a bowl and whisk them randomly.

3. Now slowly add 8 oz. grated apples and continue stirring with a rubber spatula.

4. Add flour and make a dense batter. Keep it aside for at least ten minutes.

5. Boil water in a saucepan which has short width in which spätzle machine can easily get fix.

6. Fry breadcrumbs in melted butter until they turn brown. Remove from flame and keep them aside to settle down.

7. Now again heat it after adding calvados. Put out flame when it remains half.

8. Add a pinch of salt in boiling water and then reduce flame to average.

9. Place spätzle makers over silver foil. Arrange lines of square containers in proper alignment.

10. One by one fill containers with batter. Now place these spätzle containers over simmering water and don't forget to remove foil. It will help the mixture to fall in boiling water.

11. Slowly shake square container along the tracks. In this way, batter will get mixed in pot. Stir it continually otherwise batter will stick to the base of the pot or lumps will form.

12. When spätzle is completely prepared, add this batter into calvados mixture using a slotted spoon.

13. Now add quirt of lemon and remaining butter in the form of four to five large pieces. Stir it well until it is mixed thoroughly and spätzle material begins to boil.

14. At the end sprinkle breadcrumbs. Furthermore, you can garnish its top with cinnamon and sugar powder or nuts.

Spätzle nuts

It is the most desirable spätzle sweet dish and usually served along with coffee or tea at supper. This dish serves also as the best snack and kids favorite as it takes less time in making and for this reason, this dish is mom's favorite too.

Serves:4

Time: 5 mins.

Ingredients:

- Eggs (2)
- Mix powder of cinnamon and sugar.
- Flour (1 cup plain)
- Oil (for frying)
- Salt (Half tbsp)
- flour (1 cup, full, self-rising)
- milk or water (1 cup)

Directions:

1. Heat the oil in a pan.

2. Mix together two types of flour. Make a soft batter in a way regular way.

3. Now make small bunches of spätzle and slowly drop them in heated oil.

4. Once they turn brown and fully cooked, soak them on paper.

5. Coat cinnamon sugar powder on them.

Conclusion

You've made it to the end! Thank you for reading through the Beginner Spätzle Recipes Cookbook. I hope you all 30 delicious & easy spätzle recipes for beginners to German cuisine.

If you enjoyed what you read through, feel free to use a few minutes to leave a review on the platform on which you purchased the book. Your feedback really helps me improve the quality of my work.

Cheers!